Garfield County Libraries
402 W. Main Street
New Castle CO 81647
www.garfieldlibraries.org
970-984-2346

My Dog's a Mommy!

by Leonie Bennett

Consultant: Mitch Cronick

BEARPORT
PUBLISHING COMPANY, INC.
New York, New York

Credits

t=top, b=bottom, c=center, l=left, r=right, OFC=outside front cover
Corbis: 4. Kaspurgold Golden Retrievers: 22b, 22t.
Kaspurgold Golden Retrievers (Phil and Susan Hocking): 5, 14, 15, 16, 17, 18, 19, 21.
Kaspurgold Golden Retrievers (Colin Seddon): 12–13, 20, 22c.
Shoonahs Golden Retrievers (Marilyn Barford): 8, 9, 10–11, 20, 22–23.
Superstock: 6-7, 23b.

Library of Congress Cataloging-in-Publication Data

Bennett, Leonie.

My dog's a mommy! / by Leonie Bennett.

  p. cm. — (I love reading)

Includes index.

ISBN 1-59716-158-6 (library binding) — ISBN 1-59716-184-5 (pbk.)

1. Puppies — Juvenile literature. 2. Dogs — Parturition — Juvenile literature. I. Title. II. Series.

SF426.5.B45 2006

636.7'07 — dc22

2005029611

For more information, write to Bearport Publishing Company, Inc., 101 Fifth Avenue, Suite 6R, New York, New York 10003. Printed in the United States of America.

1 2 3 4 5 6 7 8 9 10

The I Love Reading series was originally developed by Tick Tock Media.

CONTENTS

My dog Molly

Molly is a golden retriever.

She is three years old.

Fat tummy

Molly has a fat tummy.

5

Going to the vet

The **vet** checks to see that Molly is **healthy**.

He looks in Molly's eyes and ears.

He feels Molly's tummy.

Molly is going to have puppies.

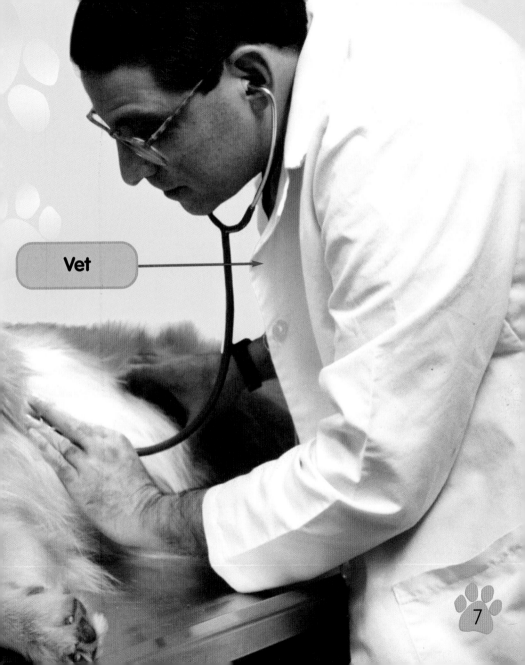

Vet

My dog's a mommy

We make a bed for Molly.

We put it in a quiet place.

Molly's bed

Blanket

Soon the puppies are born.

Ten puppies

There are ten puppies
in the **litter**.

Molly licks them clean.

The puppies drink milk from Molly.

Then they go to sleep.

The new puppies

The puppies are two days old.

They can't see.

They can't walk.

They sleep a lot.

The puppies sleep close together to keep warm.

Growing up

Now the puppies are four weeks old.

They can see.

They can walk.

The puppies
sleep in a
big box.

The puppies
want to get
out of the box.

Time for dinner

Now the puppies are eight weeks old.

They can eat **solid** food.

This puppy is the biggest.

He eats a lot.

The puppies still drink milk from Molly.

Playful puppies

The puppies like to play.

They like
to chew.

They like
to chase.

18

Sometimes the puppies have
accidents on the floor.

The puppies
still sleep a lot.

Saying good-bye

Now the puppies are ten weeks old.

It is time to say good-bye to one of them.

This puppy is going to a loving
new home.

21

Glossary

healthy
(HEL-thee)
not ill

litter (LIT-ur)
a group of
animals born
at the same time

solid (SOL-id)
something
hard and firm

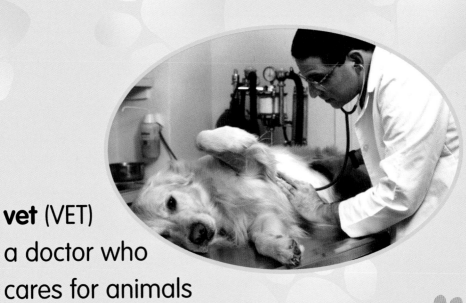

vet (VET)
a doctor who
cares for animals

Index

Learn More

Cole, Joanna. *My Puppy Is Born.* New York: Mulberry Books (1991).

DK Publishing. *Puppy (Watch Me Grow).* New York: DK Publishing (2005).

www.animaland.org/asp/petcare/dog411.asp

www.pbs.org/wnet/nature/puppies/photoessay.html